Original title:
Whispers of the Tropical Breeze

Copyright © 2025 Creative Arts Management OÜ
All rights reserved.

Author: Benjamin Caldwell
ISBN HARDBACK: 978-1-80581-473-3
ISBN PAPERBACK: 978-1-80581-000-1
ISBN EBOOK: 978-1-80581-473-3

Secrets Beneath the Canopy

A monkey juggles fruit with flair,
While parrots gossip without a care.
They aim for the fruits, but hit a shoe,
Laughter echoes as the chaos grew.

The sloth dreams of a race in vain,
While the jaguar thinks he's quite the brain.
But all the while, the lizards cheer,
'You'll win, oh sloth, next year, my dear!'

Breezes in the Banyan Shade

A breeze tickles leaves, they dance around,
The turtles giggle, lost and found.
Under the shade, the frogs prepare,
To leap in sync like they just don't care!

A bee buzzes in, wants to join the show,
But lands on a snail, oh no, oh no!
With laughter shared, the antics fly,
While squirrels debate, 'Should we try to fly?'

Swaying Tales of the Tropical Night

The moon peeks down on a sleepy vine,
As fireflies waltz, their glow divine.
A crab complains it missed the dance,
'My timing stinks, I had no chance!'

The owl hoots loud, requests a beat,
While palm trees sway in a rhythm neat.
But all agree, in vibrant glee,
'Next time, dear crab, come join the spree!'

Soft Songs from the Shore

Waves come crashing with a happy cheer,
While shells play music that all can hear.
A dolphin flips with a flair so bright,
'Catch me if you can, I'm out of sight!'

Seagulls squawk in a sing-along,
As crabs do the crabwalk to the song.
All of nature joins, with joy so pure,
'Let's dance on the shore, who could want more?'

The Language of Gentle Waters

The river chuckles as it flows,
Fish wear glasses, striking poses.
Turtles gossip on the rocks,
While frogs croak out their funny jokes.

Dance of ducks in fancy shoes,
They gossip on the latest news.
Water's edge, where tales unfold,
Each splash is laughter, pure and bold.

Echoes of the Coastal Sky

The gulls are squawking, what a sight,
Sharing secrets in morning light.
Crabs parade with funny hats,
As waves tickle their silly backs.

Sandcastles wink in playful glee,
With moats full of giggles and tea.
The sun's a jester, warm and bright,
Making shadows dance with delight.

Swaying Rhythms of Wildflowers

Petals giggle in the breeze,
Bees throw parties among the trees.
Butterflies boast of their best moves,
As daisies sway in fanciful grooves.

Ladybugs have a parade in line,
In polka dots, they twirl and shine.
With nature's tune, they jump and spin,
Laughing hard, they let the fun begin.

The Hidden Love of Sea and Sky

When the sun kisses the ocean's face,
Fish make funny splashes, pick up pace.
Clouds shape hearts, a love so grand,
As the breeze conducts with a gentle hand.

Raindrops play hide and seek with sand,
While seashells offer stories, unplanned.
Together they giggle, in playful strife,
Nature's jesters, spreading joy in life.

Rustling Leaves in a Sunlit Glade

In a glade where squirrels play,

Leaves rustle, they say hooray!

A snake slips by in a dazzling bow,

Then trips on roots, oh what a show!

A parrot laughs, it's quite the scene,

Telling tales that are rarely seen.

A frog leaps in, what's that splash?

He joins the dance, a wild, wet bash!

Sunlight dapples their zany spree,

Chasing shadows like you and me.

Life's a game, they hop and spin,

In this glade where fun won't thin!

Melodies of the Coral Coves

At coral coves where seashells ring,

Fish form bands, serenading spring.

A crab sings low, a snail hums loud,

Together, they form a wobbly crowd!

A starfish strums a rocky base,

While octopuses dance in place.

The clownfish joke with every flip,

As dolphins join with a cartoon skip!

The waves keep time with a gentle clap,

As sea turtles take a cozy nap.

Every splash brings giggles bright,

In coral coves, the world's all right!

Whispers Among the Fronds

Among the fronds, a secret buzz,

A toucan chats, "Let's cause a fuzz!"

A lizard grins, tail in a twist,

"Join the party, you can't resist!"

Frogs in tuxedos hop with flair,

While sloths sway without a care.

"Hold my vine!" the monkey shouts,

As snacks roll in, oh what a rout!

In this place where laughter grows,

The party never comes to close.

Leaves sway with every silly jest,

Among the fronds, it's quite the fest!

A Dance with the Ocean's Breath

Beneath the sun, where the waves do prance,

Sand crabs burst into a quirky dance.

The tide rolls in with a playful tease,

While shells giggle in the gentle breeze.

A fish pops up with a cheeky grin,

"Bet I can dive faster, let's begin!"

The seagulls squawk, "They're all so slow!"

As they whirl around in the ocean's show.

With every wave, a joke is made,

As starfish mime in the sun's parade.

In this seaside bash, no one feels blue,

It's a dance of joy, just me and you!

Promises Kept in the Air

The parrot says, 'Where's my snack?'
Loudly squawking from a tree's back.
The breeze giggles, playing tricks,
While monkeys throw their silly sticks.

A crab's dance on the sunlit shore,
His tiny moves, we can't ignore.
With every flip, he takes a bow,
'Look at me! I'm here, right now!'

The coconut falls with a big boom,
Making everyone jump in their zoom.
The fish below just laugh and grin,
As they wait for the splash from within.

Seagulls squawk, "Did you see that?"
While a beach ball flies, splat-splat-splat.
Promises made here in the sun,
Let's keep this laughter, just for fun!

Hidden Stories in the Coral Sands

In the grains where secrets hide,
A hermit crab is full of pride.
He wears a shell that's quite the sight,
Reflecting sunlight, oh so bright.

Underwater gardens sway and dance,
Creatures prance in a silly trance.
The sea turtles let out a snore,
While sea cucumbers haunt the floor.

Starfish gossip on the reef's edge,
'Did you hear? That fish won a pledge!'
Sand dollars pass notes, sharing gossip,
While dolphins leap, their flips nonstop.

With each tide, stories swirl and spin,
Of treasures found, and secrets within.
So come, my friend, join the beachy spree,
Where laughter echoes, wild and free!

Rhythms of Nature's Breath

The palm trees sway with a happy jig,
While a beach ball rolls like a big pig.
To the rhythm of the surf's sweet play,
All nature joins the dance today.

A cricket chirps a catchy song,
While the sun bathes us all day long.
The waves keep clapping, what a show,
As all creatures join in the flow.

Breezes tickle as they flit and fly,
Carrying laughter, oh my, oh my!
A turtle's grin is quite the sight,
As he wiggles back to delight.

In this chaos, joy does flow,
Nature's tunes are on with a glow.
Let's tap our feet to the sandy beat,
And dance along, what a summer treat!

The Gentle Touch of Ocean Air

A jellyfish drifts with a flair,
Softly floating in ocean air.
With tentacles that wave and sway,
He jokes, 'I'm just here for the play!'

The sunbeams tickle, warm and light,
While crabby friends engage in a fight.
They shuffle sideways, 'Who wants to play?'
In this wild and whacky display.

Waves tumble softly like a yawn,
As seaweed weaves like a green pawn.
The gulls overhead, they cheer and dive,
Making sure all the fun's alive.

Ocean whispers secrets untold,
Of clams that pretend to be bold.
In this zany coastal affair,
Every moment's a cause for player's flair!

Tropical Whispers in the Mist

In the morning fog, a coconut sighs,
A parrot quips, while the monkey flies.
Palm trees giggle, dancing in the breeze,
Tickling the aunts and the buzzing bees.

Frogs in tuxedos jump to the beat,
While sand crabs salsa with two little feet.
Laughter echoes through the leafy lanes,
As lizards play chess using two sugarcanes.

Hints of the Golden Horizon

A sunbeam tickles the ocean's face,
While fish blow bubbles in a silly race.
Seagulls wearing shades stroll the sidewalk,
Crabs on a bench share gossip and talk.

Coconuts giggle, rolling down the shore,
Chatting with shells as they just implore.
Laughter spills over the golden glow,
As waves do the limbo, putting on a show.

Dance of Shadows on the Sands

Footprints cha-cha along the sun-kissed trail,
Where shadows twirl in a lighthearted gale.
Sand castles wobble, their turrets will sway,
As crabs do a jig, come join the ballet.

Kites in the sky make curious spins,
While children giggle at their silly sins.
With ice cream in hand, they make a grand mess,
The heat doesn't stop them; they dance nonetheless.

Murmured Invitations of the Jungle

In the thick of the vines, a toucan unplugs,
Laughing at sloths, those slow little bugs.
Monkeys share puns, swinging from the trees,
While jaguars giggle and play hide and tease.

The frogs throw a party near the cool stream,
With goodies galore that'll make you just beam.
Each rustle and rumble a call to the fun,
The jungle awaits, let the laughter run!

Hush of the Hibiscus

In bright hues the petals play,
They gossip in a colorful way.
A bold bloom with a silly pose,
Daring the bees to come and doze.

A butterfly slips, oh what a sight,
Giggling as it takes flight.
Swaying softly to a tune,
Dancing with charm beneath the moon.

Laughter rustles through the leaves,
Creating mischief, oh how it weaves.
The garden's a stage for nature's jest,
A funny show that never rests.

So come, join in on this floral cheer,
Where every bloom is filled with cheer.
In this patch of paradise, so divine,
The playful petals daintily entwine.

Echoes of the Island Heart

On shores where laughter meets the sand,
A crab scuttles in a silly band.
He sidesteps with a quirky flair,
Chasing shells without a care.

The coconuts chuckle on high,
As breezes pause to wonder why.
A parrot squawks a cheeky joke,
In hues so bright, it seems to poke.

Flip-flops flapping, tourists rush,
Tripping over waves with a blush.
Splashing water, grins abound,
A symphony of fun is found.

With every tide, a new giggle forms,
Creating delight in playful storms.
Stay awhile, let worries part,
In this place, we share our heart.

Gentle Sighs of the Coastline

The sun slips down in a lazy way,
Tickling the waves of the bay.
A dolphin darts with a playful toss,
In its wake, giggles it emboss.

Seagulls squawk, with attitude bold,
Stealing fries, oh, what a gold!
They dance on currents with much glee,
As if they've conquered the salty sea.

Inflatable flamingos float on by,
With sunglasses perched, so fly!
They nod along to the beachside band,
Making everyone laugh on the sand.

So let the tides tickle your toes,
And let the funny ocean flows.
With every wave, there's delight anew,
On this coast where laughter grew.

Caress of the Warm Currents

The current whispers a silly tale,
Of fish in hats that ride the gale.
They wiggle and giggle, swim with flair,
In waters that echo laughter rare.

A sea turtle claims the water's path,
With a grin that sparks the ocean's wrath.
He's got swim trunks, they're very tight,
Before him, the waves take flight.

Shells clack and chatter on the shore,
Telling tales of days before.
The tide rolls in, tickles your feet,
As if the ocean's trying to compete.

Drifting off to a goofy beat,
Where breezes play on joyful repeat.
So dance along, let worries cease,
In warm currents, surely, find peace.

Secrets among the Mangroves

In the mangroves, secrets hide,
Where crabs practice their samba glide.
The iguanas gossip in leafy chairs,
While fish debate their long-lost wares.

A parrot squawks with a wobbly jest,
"Why did the snail wear a fancy vest?"
Tangled roots sway, unpredictable dance,
Even the mudfish seem to prance.

Laughter echoes through the twisted trees,
As turtles sing songs that float on the breeze.
A hidden world where silliness reigns,
In a realm where logic takes playful chains.

Among the mangroves, great and small,
Every creature is a comedian's call.
With a jig and a wig, they celebrate life,
In this quirky, green, and whimsical strife.

Language of the Sunlit Breezes

The sunlit breeze plays on the shore,
A mischievous whisper, who could ask for more?
It tickles the toes of a dozing cat,
While sandcastles giggle under a hat.

Seagulls squawk with a haughty flair,
"Do you really think sunlight is fair?"
With feathers ruffled and beaks so bright,
They squabble over snacks in a comical fight.

Crabs in sunglasses stroll with style,
With tiny reflections, they pause for a while.
"Is it too sunny or just our party?"
They chuckle, wiggling, while acting hearty.

The beach is alive with shenanigans abound,
Where laughter and sand are always found.
The language of breezes, tales we spin,
With each gust of wind, let the fun begin!

Sighs of the Coral Coast

On the coral coast, the waves do sigh,
"Why don't fish learn to fly?"
They splash and flip, what a silly sight,
As dolphins leap, taking off in delight.

The anemone blooms with a wink,
"Did you hear? The seaweed can think!"
With tentacles dancing like old-time pros,
They share their jokes while the current flows.

Starfish lounge, counting their toes,
In sweet ocean dreams, nobody knows.
"If I had legs, I'd dance like a fool!"
They giggle together, breaking the rule.

A crab in a shell hosts a wild bash,
With sea cucumbers offering a splash.
The coral coast hums with eccentricity,
A watery world of comedic mystery.

Enchanted Winds of the South

From the south, the winds come flirty,
Flapping like shirts that smell quite dirty.
They tickle the cheeks of the laughing trees,
And chase after clouds that drift with ease.

Lizards lounge, complaining of heat,
"Why run from the wind? It offers a seat!"
With sun hats balanced upon their crew,
The lizards laugh loud with impeccable view.

At sunset, each breeze tells a joke,
The kind that makes you laugh 'til you choke.
"How does the ocean stay in its chair?"
With surfboards, it answers, "I don't care!"

Enchanted winds swirl in a circus ballet,
Whirling the flowers in a bright display.
In the south, where the breezes jest,
Life's a party—just come as a guest!

Murmurs of Sun-Drenched Horizons

Sunlight dances on the bay,
Fishes joke, they swim and sway.
Crabs wear hats, quite out of place,
While seagulls laugh and join the race.

Coconuts gossip on the trees,
Telling tales of salty seas.
Each breeze tickles, a playful tease,
As laughter bounces, all with ease.

Boughs that Whisper and Sing

Coconuts giggle, swinging low,
Branches sway, putting on a show.
Frogs in hats hop with delight,
They leap and dance through day and night.

Parrots squawk in silly tones,
Sharing secrets to the stones.
Every leaf has jokes to share,
In the sun, they banter and care.

The Lulling Tide's Embrace

Waves come in with a soft pat,
Chasing clams where crabs do chat.
Turtles giggle, rolling by,
Snapping shells with a playful sigh.

Starfish lounge on sandy beds,
Telling jokes of sleepyheads.
Dolphins tease with joyful clicks,
In the tide's embrace, there's always tricks.

Chasing Shadows Under the Palms

Shadows play hide and seek with light,
While ants march on like a funny sight.
Palms sway like they're in a dance,
Lost in rhythm, they take a chance.

The breeze tells tales of silly dreams,
Of ice cream sundaes and chocolate creams.
Laughter echoes beneath the sky,
As playful breezes swirl and fly.

Tranquility in the Canopy

In the trees, a parrot squawks,
Telling tales of distant walks,
Sipping nectar, bees go buzz,
While monkeys swing with playful fuzz.

Lizards sunning on a log,
Ribbiting right with a froggy dog,
Coconuts drop, a thud, a roll,
As squirrels scamper, feeling whole.

Mangoes burst with a juicy grin,
While crickets hum their silly din,
A sloth hangs loose with a lazy yawn,
As butterflies dance till the dawn.

Each leaf giggles with a breeze,
In this canopy of fun and tease,
Where every creature finds its groove,
Nature's laugh, a tropical move.

Sunlit Echoes of the Hidden Shore.

Underneath the palm fronds sway,
A crab in red does the cha-cha play,
Seagulls dive in a feathery race,
While sunbathers hide from a splashy face.

The waves tickle toes in retreat,
Chasing shells, oh what a feat,
Sandcastles built, lopsided and tall,
With a proud flag made of a scrap, no small.

Jellyfish dance, a wobbly sight,
With flip-flops flying left and right,
The ocean whispers a salty joke,
As dolphins giggle, in laughter, cloak.

In this hidden cove so fine,
Where sun and laughter intertwine,
Every splash tells a seaside tale,
As joy rides high on the ocean's gale.

Gentle Secrets of the Sea

In the tide, sea turtles race,
Playing tag at a sprightly pace,
Starfish giggle, do the twist,
While fish perform in a coral mist.

A sea cucumber takes a bow,
In snazzy attire, wow wow wow,
Giant clams snicker, wide and bold,
As waves tickle, stories unfold.

Sand dollars roll with a cheeky grin,
While bubbles pop, let the fun begin,
A pelican drops his prized catch,
For a nearby pelican, oh what a match!

Under the waves, the laughter flows,
In depths where silliness grows,
Every splash and wave a song,
In the sea where friends belong.

Murmurs Beneath the Palms

Under palms, a party starts,
Where lizards play their tiny parts,
A raccoon brings a funky beat,
As fireflies flash their own retreat.

The wind tells tales of goofy glee,
A sloth goes hip with a cup of tea,
Frangipani scents the night,
With owls hooting, oh what a sight!

A turtle snaps a selfie alone,
As frogs croak their catchy tone,
With twinkling stars that twirl and sway,
This jamboree will never fray.

In the moonlight, laughter rings,
Among the leaves where adventure sings,
Underneath the palms so fine,
Life's a joke—sweet punchline.

Tales from the Rainforest Hideaway

In the jungle where the monkeys swing,
A toucan yells, 'Come hear me sing!'
The sloth just snores, in his lazy way,
While the tree frogs plot to steal the day.

A parrot squawks, 'I'm grand and neat!'
But the iguana thinks it's time to eat.
The vines all giggle, oh what a sight,
As the sun dips low, they dance in delight.

Down by the river, the piranhas play,
Teasing each other, in a fishy fray.
But the playful otter steals the scene,
With the finest splash you've ever seen!

Though the rain may fall, it brings a cheer,
For every drop brings laughter near.
In this hideaway, the stories fly,
With cheeky grins, from earth to sky.

The Language of Fluttering Wings

Butterflies flutter, in colors so bold,
As they gossip about the flowers they hold.
The bees buzz in, like a buzzing band,
"Stop stealing nectar, you're under a hand!"

A hummingbird zips, fast and bright,
Chasing the sun, in sheer delight.
"Catch me if you can!" she chirps with glee,
While the dragonfly snickers, "You'll never see me!"

Together they swirl, a dance in the air,
Laughing at the ants, scurrying with care.
"Where's the party?" an owl hoots loud,
They all giggle softly, "In the flower crowd!"

As dusk begins to wrap its arms wide,
The birds all settle, and dreams abide.
But they'll be back to play and tease,
In the language of laughter and fluttering breeze.

Heartbeats of the Island Spirit

On the shore where the palm fronds sway,
A crab declares, 'It's my lucky day!'
While the seagulls squawk, 'We own this place!'
Stealing sandwiches with a cheeky grace.

The turtles race, in a slow-motion tease,
"Fastest in the sea!" says the fish with ease.
But behind them all, with a sly little grin,
The octopus plots for a snappy win!

The sunsets paint a colorful tale,
As the waves sing a playful gale.
And the island spirit hums a tune,
Under the watchful eye of the moon.

So gather 'round, let the laughter bloom,
In this paradise, there's always room.
With heartbeats of joy, the night will end,
As dreams of the island begin to blend.

The Essence of a Gentle Zephyr

A breeze dances low, tickling the leaves,
"Excuse me!" says the flower, "But don't you tease!"
The palm trees sway, with a chuckle so grand,
As the wind tells tales of far-off land.

The squirrel jumps high, chasing the airflow,
"Watch me!" he squeaks, but he tumbles so slow.
The breeze just giggles, "Better luck next time!"
As the island hums to a tropical rhyme.

A few dandelions join in for fun,
Blowing seeds everywhere, oh what a run!
While the sun dips low, wrapping all in gold,
The laughter echoes, a sight to behold.

So let the gentle winds stir up some cheer,
For on this island, the joy is near.
In the dance of the breeze, let's twirl and spin,
And share in the smiles, as the night begins.

Murmurs from the Deep Blue

Underwater giggles in the sea,
Fish are laughing, can't you see?
Octopuses dance with fancy shoes,
Crabs are cracking jokes, lightening blues.

A dolphin slides by with a splashy grin,
Sardines wiggle, they can't help but spin.
"Hey mate!" says a turtle with a wink,
"Life's a party, pour me a drink!"

Currents twist, a parade for all,
Seaweed sways, making the call.
A seagull swoops down with flair,
"Why're you swimming? There's snacks up there!"

Jellyfish giggle, bouncing with glee,
"Float with us, you'll feel so free!"
They bounce and jig, a sea-bound crew,
In the ocean's laugh, let's join in too!

Sighs of the Emerald Canopy

Leaves are chatting, such silly gossip,
Vines are twirling, they're doing a flip.
The parrot squawks jokes, oh what a clown,
Swinging from branches, upside down!

A monkey peers down, throws down a nut,
"Hey, grasshoppers, what's with that strut?"
Butterflies giggle in colors bright,
Spreading their wings, making it light.

A lizard croons, like a rockstar in green,
Feeling so cool, what a wild scene!
"Let's start a band!" calls a cheeky frog,
"Bring your best beats, we'll dance in the fog!"

Rain drizzles down, giving a cheer,
Puddles reflect, "Let's jump in here!"
In the overture of playful breeze,
Nature's laughter flows with such ease!

Currents of Joy and Rest

Peppery breezes tickle your skin,
Laughter's the game, let's all dive in!
The hammock sways, a cozy retreat,
While coconuts roll, giving a beat.

Friends gather 'round with silly grins,
Telling tall tales of past monkey sins.
"Remember the time that crab lost his pants?"
"Oh yes! He danced like he had two left hands!"

A toucan croons, "I can sing too!"
"Sure, but a disco ball? Need a clue!"
In sunshine, they spin, hop, and sway,
In warm currents, they frolic and play.

Time drips slowly, just like the sun,
Every moment, just look at the fun!
With laughter and joy, let worries flee,
In this paradise, we're forever free!

The Language of Tidal Songs

Ocean waves hum with a silly beat,
Crabs are the drummers, tapping their feet.
Seagulls are squawking in perfect tune,
Echoes of laughter beneath the moon.

Starfish join in with their own wild jam,
"Hey, don't forget us!" they shout, "We're glam!"
As jellyfish pulse in neon delight,
It's a bubble party, oh what a sight!

Barnacles lean in, shushing the moans,
"Keep it down, we're trying to phone!"
While clams clack rhythm, shells open wide,
Dance with the tide, let worries slide!

In this grand concert where the sea meets the sky,
Every creature's invited, just give it a try.
So laugh with the waves, let your spirits soar,
In this tidal wonder, there's always more!

Laughter of the Surf

The waves tickle toes, oh what a game,
As sea foam giggles, it calls out my name.
With every splash, the ocean just grins,
It splatters my laughter, inviting more wins.

A crab in a hurry, scuttles away,
Chasing after shells like it's part of the play.
Seagulls squawk funny, they dance in the sky,
While fishing for snacks, they flail with a sigh.

The sun takes a dip, all dressed up in gold,
But don't be fooled, it's just feeling bold.
Flip-flops are flopping, a comical feat,
As everyone stumbles, oh what a treat!

Here on the shore, where the laughter rings,
Every clumsy step, just adds to the springs.
So let's make a splash, dive into the fun,
Beneath the hot rays, we laugh till we're done!

Harmonies of the Swaying Seaweeds

The seaweed's dancing, it's having a ball,
With tentacles waving, it's having a thrall.
They sway and shimmied, all covered in sand,
Making the ocean a funky band.

An octopus twirls, in a grand ballet,
While fish join the chorus, they sing all day.
They flip and they flop, in a colorful show,
Even clams start to clap, they're putting on a glow.

The jellyfish stings, but only in jest,
"Don't take it too hard!" it laughs with the rest.
As waves form a rhythm, our hearts skip a beat,
The sea's silly sounds can't be beat!

So let's join the fun, as we jig in delight,
And dance with the sea, from morning to night.
For every chuckle and every cool breeze,
Life's better when we giggle 'neath swaying seas!

Fluttering Leaves in Delight

In the jungle green, the leaves start to sway,
They giggle and jive, in a breezy ballet.
With each little flutter, they tell us a joke,
As monkeys swing by, in their playful cloak.

The parrots are squawking, in colors so bright,
Each one trying hard, to outshine the light.
They pose on a branch, with a flair and a wink,
As they laugh at the flowers which start to blush pink.

The flowers reply with a fragrant burst,
Tickled by breezes, they quench their great thirst.
A bee buzzes by, all dizzy and daft,
Chasing its own tail, oh what a good laugh!

So join in the frolic, let spirits take flight,
In this leafy arena, where humor ignites.
For nature's a joker, it tickles our souls,
In delight we will dance, where laughter unfolds!

Echoes of Silken Nights

Beneath the moonlight, the stars start to giggle,
As shadows dance slow, they twist and they wiggle.
The night is alive with a chuckle and cheer,
While crickets play tunes that are funny to hear.

Fireflies twinkle like little bright clowns,
They flit through the air, exchanging their crowns.
While owls make wise jokes, perched up on a tree,
Each hoot sends a wave of contagious glee.

The breeze tickles cheeks, as it whispers secrets,
Of midnight mischief, odd food and regrets.
A raccoon in mischief, with snacks all around,
Tiptoes through laughter, making not a sound.

So gather your friends, let's revel tonight,
In echoes of joy, let our spirits take flight.
With skies full of stars and hearts full of fun,
Life's a whimsical dance, and we've only begun!

Lilting Echoes at Daybreak

The roosters crow, but so do I,
A dancing chicken steals the pie.
Palm trees sway with a cheeky grin,
As morning starts, let the fun begin.

The sun peeks through, all golden light,
Lizards strut, an amusing sight.
A parrot laughs, it seems to tease,
While sipping juice with the buzzing bees.

Coconuts roll with a playful bounce,
As monkeys swing, they twist and pounce.
The ocean chuckles, waves with glee,
In this wild party, come dance with me!

So grab a hat, and let's explore,
This charming land, it's never a bore.
With laughter ringing, we'll romp and play,
In this sunny world, let's seize the day!

Glistening Whispers of the Lagoon

A frog in boots jumps by with flair,
While dragonflies swoop down in air.
The water shimmers, a giggling stream,
As turtles plot their grand scheme.

Fish wear hats; they fancy their dress,
Trying to impress? Oh, what a mess!
The ripples dance to an unseen song,
In this hilarious place, you can't go wrong.

Crabs do the cha-cha on the shore,
While seaweed wiggles, demanding more.
And there's a crab with a joke in queue,
'Why did the barnacle get a shoe?'

Each splash a laugh, each wave a cheer,
In our lagoon of joy, we persevere.
Come join the fun, let your worries glide,
Where the sun meets the sea, let's take a ride!

Tails of the Petals in the Breeze

Petals float, like little kites,
Dancing on air, oh what delights!
A dog named Benny tries to chase,
Smacking his tail in a wild race.

The flowers gossip, but I can't hear,
With bees that buzz, all bringing cheer.
A curious cat, on a branch she sits,
Watching the antics, while thinking wits.

A squirrel debates, is it time to nap?
Or grab some fruit before a trap?
Nature chuckles, with mischief abound,
In this floral circus, joy is found.

So let's toast to petals, to tails and fun,
In this merry chaos, we smile as one.
With each silly twist, let laughter seize,
In our garden with joy, dancing in the breeze!

The Songbird's Call at Dusk

As the sun dips low, what's that sound?
A bird's high note, soaring around.
He sings of pizza, a feast on a tree,
Join in the chorus, come sing with me.

The crickets join in, the frogs agree,
It's quite the harmonious jubilee.
A sly raccoon peeks out for a snack,
With a pizza slice, he just won't lack.

The moon takes a bow, a shining show,
As fireflies flicker, a soft glow.
Each note a giggle, the night grows bright,
In this quirky concert, everything's right.

So let's sway to the tunes of dusk's embrace,
In this whimsical world, there's always space.
For laughter and joy beneath the stars,
Raise your glass high and cheers from afar!

Notes of Ferns in the Wind

In the jungle, ferns do giggle,
A lizard sneezes, then cools its wiggle.
Ladybugs dance, so bright and spry,
They tip their hats as they flit by.

Coconuts chuckle, up in a tree,
They think they're kings, so carefree.
The monkeys howl, a merry band,
Stealing fruit with a cheeky hand.

The parrot squawks, "What's that sound?"
A blowfish floats, and it spins around.
Each leaf tells tales, a laugh in disguise,
Nature's own comedy, to our surprise.

Through the breeze, the jokes take flight,
Tickling the palm trees, oh what a sight!
With each gentle rustle, our worries cease,
In this tropical realm, we find our peace.

Breezes of a Forgotten Island

On an island where crabs wear shoes,
They strut around, sharing their news.
Pineapples giggle in the sun,
They claim that life is just pure fun.

Seagulls squabble over a feast,
While a turtle complains, "I'm the least!"
Each wave a whisper, a playful tease,
Swaying the palm trees with utmost ease.

A coconut drops, "Watch out below!"
It's comedy hour with quite the show.
As the island chuckles, a smile takes hold,
Tales of the silly, both new and old.

In the breeze, laughter's the thread,
We weave our stories, joking instead.
Together we sway, with the humor of fate,
On this quirky island, oh can't we relate?

Secrets in the Flowers' Hearts

In the garden where daisies plot,
The bees make jokes, oh what a lot!
Petunias gossip, with colors so bright,
About the roses' recent fright.

Tulips twirl under the sun's warm gaze,
Telling puns in a fragrant haze.
Butterflies crack up, they can't take a pause,
With every flutter, they cause applause.

Sunflowers wink as they oh so tower,
"A little sun never dims our power!"
Meanwhile, the pansies share their best lore,
Of where the best nectar flows evermore.

In these blooms, humor finds its way,
With petals chuckling throughout the day.
In every secret, a laugh we find,
Nature's joke book, beautifully aligned.

The Warmth of Distant Shores

On distant shores where sand gets tossed,
Seashells chatter, never lost.
Starfish laugh as they soak the rays,
Turning the tides into silly plays.

Waves come in, bringing a funk,
As dolphins dance, full of spunk.
The crabs have formed their own parade,
As laughter fills the sunny glade.

Coconuts roll, "Don't leave me behind!"
As they join the fun—a quirky kind.
Sun and surf, a comedic sketch,
With endless stories that we'll etch.

Together we bask in the daylight's glee,
In this warm embrace, we laugh so free.
With every ripple, a jest takes flight,
On distant shores, our hearts feel light.

Breath of the Tropical Dawn

In the morning light, the parrots squawk,
They argue over who gets the best rock.
Coconuts fall with a clunk and a plop,
While folks in hammocks just lazily flop.

The palm fronds wave like a friendly hand,
As tourists complain about too much sand.
The sun peek-a-boos, it's quite the tease,
While roosters crow with absolute ease.

Underneath a tree, a cat takes a nap,
Dreaming of fish and a cozy lap.
But that sound is just a kid with a kite,
Oh, the chaos! It's pure delight!

So grab a drink, with a tiny umbrella,
Join this wild party, you jolly fella!
With laughter and giggles, the morning starts,
In this wacky land that will capture your heart.

Lullabies on the Ocean's Edge

The waves hum a tune, soft as a dream,
While crabs play tag in a sandy scheme.
A starfish wiggles, thinking it's cool,
While a dolphin leaps, just breaking the rule.

Shells on the shore have stories to tell,
Of fish and their pranks, oh, isn't that swell?
Seagulls squawk songs, they're quite the crooners,
Who knew feathery friends could be such swooners?

But wait, there's a guy with a bucket and net,
He's determined to catch that silly pet.
A fish glares back, then gives a big splash,
Sending him stumbling, a comical crash!

As night falls, the beach begins to glow,
With laughter and music, the good vibes flow.
In this watery world where silliness reigns,
You'll find joy and giggles, forget all your pains.

Serenade of the Sunlit Shores

The sun struts high, like it owns the sky,
While surfers tumble, oh my, oh my!
A crab in a swimsuit looks ready to play,
As beachgoers shout, 'Hey! Look that way!'

Beach balls soar like they're on a spree,
A runaway flip-flop just missed a bee.
Sandy toes dancing, they wiggle and twist,
As the shore puts on its comedic twist.

A seagull steals fries from a child's small feast,
With a cheeky caw, he's quite the little beast.
Sandcastles crumble with every big wave,
While giggles erupt, oh how they misbehave!

As the sun dips low, the laughter won't stop,
The tide rolls in, showcasing a plop.
In this jolly cove where joy fills the air,
Every moment's a treasure, beyond compare.

Tender Tides of the Paradisiacal Land

The breeze carries tales from the coconut trees,
While monkeys conspire to tickle with ease.
A tourist gets splashed, what a funny sight,
As a wave roars in with all its might!

Sipping on juice, a parrot squawks loud,
Dancing on branches, it's drawing a crowd.
With laughter enveloping the colorful scene,
Life here is silly, if you know what I mean!

Flip-flops are lost in a race on the shore,
Chasing each other, who needs a chore?
A jellyfish floats, it's a noble jelly,
While kids splash around, no time to be smelly!

As nightfall approaches, the stars twinkle bright,
The laughter continues, till the morning light.
In this land of delight where joy kisses you,
Every minute's an adventure, something new.

Secrets Beneath the Starry Sky

Under the stars, a dance begins,
Tropical insects don their chins.
In laughter, the crabs make their way,
As if moonlit sand was their ballet.

Fish jump high, like they're in a game,
Splashing around, it's never the same.
The coconut falls, like a crown gone rogue,
And starfish cheer, "We're the dance prologue!"

The night brings jokes, the waves play along,
Even the seaweed hums a song.
A parrot squawks, "I'm an opera star!"
While the shells giggle, saying, "How bizarre!"

Flip-flops dance, their owners unaware,
As dolphins peek, saying, "What a fair!"
The stars above giggle, twinkling bright,
Joining in on this hilarious night.

Sweets of the Ocean's Embrace

Tropical treats lie in warm array,
Mangoes mischief, plotting how to play.
Coconuts laugh, "We're a hard-shelled crew!"
While jellyfish wiggle, saying, "Try our stew!"

Seagulls squabble for crumbs on the sand,
"A piece of pie?" they shout, oh so grand!
The ocean waves giggle, busting a myth,
"Dessert's in the sea, just take a whiff!"

An octopus twirls with sugar and spice,
"I'm the dessert chef, not once but thrice!"
A crab lifts his claws, "I'll serve you well,
With fruit and some salsa, we'll cast a spell!"

Under the sun, the laughter persists,
With sandy ice cream, no one resists.
"Who knew the ocean was so full of treats?"
Squeals of delight from the happy beach bleats!

Soft Light on a Serene Shore

Morning sun yawns, and light starts to play,
Casting shadows where kelp likes to sway.
A puppy runs wild, chasing its tail,
While crabs dig tunnels, planning a sale.

The gentle waves whisper silly rhymes,
Tickling toes as they dance through the times.
Seashells gather, dressed up for the gala,
While seaweed teases, "There's no need for drama!"

Flip-flops squeak in a wonderful tune,
While seagulls trade jokes with the bright afternoon.
A kite takes flight, giving everyone cheer,
Even the sandcastles join in the leer!

The sun sets low, laughing with glee,
As beach balls bounce with surprising decree.
"Tomorrow brings fun!" the horizon quips,
As everyone dreams of sandier trips.

Palms Bowing to the Sea

Palms swing low, like they're in a sway,
Telling the ocean, "You're here to stay!"
A lizard spikes up, ready to groove,
While the breeze nudges leaves, starting to move.

A bear-shaped floatie takes center stage,
While lifeguards snicker, not acting their age.
"Catch me if you can!" yells a fish in glee,
And a dolphin pipes up, "Join me for tea!"

The clouds overhead chuckle and tease,
"Why not untie and float with the breeze?"
While palmtrees bend, relaxed in their dance,
The beachgoers bask in a lazy romance.

As twilight descends on the fun-filled shore,
The moon winks, "I've seen this magic before!"
In the heart of the night, joy lays its claim,
To the sweet, salty air and playful acclaim.

Notes of the Sweltering Canopy

Under the leaves, the parrots squawk,
A symphony of chatter, like pure sock.
Monkeys swing with grace and a splash,
While beetles dance, making quite the clash.

The lizards lounge, sunbathing bright,
In a game of tag, they just take flight.
Coconuts drop without a heed,
As if they're playing, 'Catch if you need!'

The sloth gives a yawn, so slow and grand,
While ants march by, all in a band.
Every creature boasts a quirky thing,
It's a rainforest party, let the fun bring!

With every rustle, oh what a scene,
Even the frogs wear a crown of green.
Nature's laughter fills the humid air,
In this wild playground, what a funny affair!

Caressing Zephyrs at Dusk

The twilight breeze tickles my nose,
As crickets serenade, in their fancy prose.
Fireflies dance like stars on the ground,
Creating a show where giggles abound.

Swaying palms, they join the fun,
Bending down as if to run.
A chameleon stuck in a game,
'Not green, not brown—what's my name?'

The moon peeks out, with a glimmering grin,
While bats take flight, oh where to begin?
The mango tree chuckles, ripe and round,
"Eat me quick, before you hit the ground!"

In this twilight realm, laughter roams wide,
Where every harmless creature takes pride.
With silly antics all around,
It's a merry chase, no need to frown!

Breathless Beauty of the Isles

Breezes glide past palm tree hair,
While seagulls squawk without a care.
Coconut crabs in a hurry to race,
Stumble and tumble—oh, what a place!

The waves slap gently, a playful tease,
While sandcastles melt with mischievous ease.
A hermit crab dressed in a shell so fine,
Parades through the beach, thinking it divine.

With every splash, a story unfolds,
Of wacky waves and treasures told.
Starfish giggle as they're flipped and spun,
Under the sun, oh, isn't this fun?

In every grain of sand, a tale so sweet,
Of silly antics where breezes meet.
From sunrise to sunset, laughter will soar,
On these playful isles, who could ask for more?

Cascading Songs of Nature

In the jungle's heart, where the loud birds sing,
A tap dance from frogs, oh what a fling!
The waterfall chatters, gossiping loud,
While the fish wiggle, showing off proud.

A squirrel with flair, in shades of gray,
Claims every nut like it's his birthday.
With every rustle, a joke takes flight,
Nature's own stand-up, pure delight!

The rustling leaves hum a tune so bright,
As butterflies flutter in sheer delight.
"Why did the bird join the circus?" they say,
"Because it wanted to learn how to play!"

Here in the wild, laughter flows free,
With creatures of all kinds, oh can't you see?
In this dazzling realm of silly surprise,
Nature's comedy stretches, oh how it flies!

Shadows of the Coconut Grove

In the shade, we dance and sway,
Coconuts laughing in a fray.
A crab in a tux, what a sight!
He joins our party, bold and bright.

Seagulls squawk with a cheeky cheer,
As we sip coconut water, have no fear.
The breeze tells jokes of far-off lands,
While palm trees wave their leafy hands.

Bikini-clad squirrels steal a snack,
They dart and dash, no time to slack.
We point and laugh, it's quite the show,
In this grove of giggles, time moves slow.

So when you hear a ticklish breeze,
Know it's just us, and we've got keys.
To unlock joy, let laughter swell,
In shadows where coconut secrets dwell.

Secrets of the Endless Summer

The sun is a prankster, plays with our hats,
Blowing them off like mischievous cats.
Flip-flops flapping, a lovely parade,
As we chase the breeze through palm-tree shade.

Ice cream melts faster than we can run,
Our laughter echoes, it's all just fun.
We charm the lizards with silly tunes,
While planning a dance with the afternoon moon.

Our secrets are whispered in sandy spells,
With seashells that giggle and tickle our shells.
Oh, the endless summer, where nonsense prevails,
We ride on the wind, with sunscreened details.

The waves have stories of dolphins that tease,
As they leap and dive with remarkable ease.
So join the fun, don't sit and glum,
In the endless summer, let laughter drum!

Chants of the Tidal Rhythm

The tide rolls in with a boisterous tune,
Waves making mischief under a full moon.
Crabs toss their shells in uproarious glee,
Chanting along with the fish in the sea.

Flip-flops go flying as waves crash near,
We giggle and scream like we have no fear.
Seashells applaud with a clap-clap cheer,
While seaweed dances to music unclear.

The ocean's a jester, always in jest,
Stirring breezes that won't let us rest.
Mermaids gossip with shells in a group,
Sharing secrets of surf in a bubbly loop.

Every splash tells a story of fun,
While jellyfish float like balloons in the sun.
So come sing along to the rhythmic spree,
Where the sea meets laughter, wild and free.

Sibilant Stories of the Surf

The surf whispers tales both silly and bright,
Of fish wearing hats, oh what a sight!
Barnacles gossip about boats that pass,
With jokes and chuckles that rival the grass.

A pelican dives in a clumsy ballet,
Splashing us all in a watery spray.
The crabs hold a meeting on sandcastles high,
Discussing their plans for a crabby sky.

Seashells chuckle as they spin in the foam,
Welcoming travelers who call it their home.
We build towers that float and pretend they can fly,
While seagulls drop in, just to say hi.

So listen closely to surf's merry song,
Where the silly stories forever belong.
Each wave a giggle, each splash a cheer,
At the coast where humor is always near.

The Caress of Warm Winds

A breeze so light tickles my nose,
It dances past, like a playful pose.
It steals my hat, oh what a theft,
I laugh and chase, it's my funny left!

The sun is bright, the palm leaves sway,
I tripped on sand, oh what a play!
The ocean whispers, "Don't you slip!"
But laughter's my only champion ship!

My drink is tipped, oh how it spills,
The wind just laughs, it has its thrills.
A pelican dives, what a clumsy bird,
I giggle loud, he must've heard!

So come and join this silly spree,
With breezy puns and salty glee.
When life gets tough, just take a chance,
And let the wind lead you in dance!

Songs of the Swaying Coconut

Coconuts sing in a swinging choir,
Their melodies dance, never tire.
One falls down, it rolls away,
I laugh out loud, what a nutty day!

Palm trees sway with a rhythm sweet,
They shake their leaves to the happy beat.
But one gusty breeze brings a ticklish bite,
I giggle and juggle like a green delight!

The crabs all scuttle, ruffled and shy,
They peek at the beach as I pass by.
They pinch my toes! Oh, what a game,
I hop and squeal, it's never the same!

So raise a glass to the coconut crew,
With funny tunes and laughter too.
In this tropical land, the joy won't cease,
We dance and chuckle, a holiday feast!

Hush of the Island Night

The stars are twinkling like a cheeky grin,
Crickets chirp softly, let the fun begin.
A firefly blinks, a tiny disco ball,
I try to catch it, but I trip and fall!

The moon whispers jokes, so witty and bright,
It tickles my brain on this silly night.
The shadows get bold and join in the fun,
They trip over rocks, oh look how they run!

A gecko hiccups, then clears its throat,
I nearly burst out in a giggling note.
The breeze tells tales of a pirate's cat,
Who stole a whole feast and wore a hat!

With every laugh, the night carries cheer,
In this hush, the humor's near.
So join the dance, let laughter resound,
For in this night, joy truly is found!

Soft Echoes in Paradise

Echoes of laughter bounce off the sea,
A parrot squawks, "Hey, look at me!"
Frisbees fly, dogs zigzag and bark,
Our picnic spread is not quite a lark!

Salty chips tumble, oh what a mess,
The breeze just giggles, "You're such a stress!"
A seagull swoops, eyeing our feast,
I wave my arms, become the least!

We fill our hearts with the sun's warm glow,
With silly pranks, like a slapstick show.
A splash in the waves, someone's wet feet,
All in good fun, what a treat to meet!

So raise your voice in joyous cheer,
With every echo, let laughter appear.
In this paradise spell, let all be free,
For a funny life is the way to be!

Sonnet of the Fading Sun

As the sun dips, it draws a big grin,
The sky wears shades of orange and pink.
A coconut laughs, it teeters with sin,
While lizards gossip, their tails made to wink.

Ghost crabs scuttle, with shells all aglow,
They dance in the sand, quite merry and spry.
The starfish hold secrets they'll never bestow,
As the day waves goodbye, with a cheeky sigh.

The sea squirrels mock, with a playful shout,
Throwing seaweed at gulls, what a sticky spree!
"Oh come join the fun!" they repeatedly shout,
But the gulls just roll eyes, it's not what they see.

So let's raise a toast, to the bold, the absurd,
To sunsets that giggle, and jest with a spark.
In the world of the silly, life often's deferred,
But we'll laugh till the dawn begins to ignite the dark.

Hushed Conversations at Twilight

Under the moon, chitchat takes flight,
Nights waltz with stars, all dressed up for fun.
Frogs croak their tales in the soft pale light,
While sloths show their moves—slow-motion rerun.

A bat flips and flaps, with gossip on pause,
"Who's got the best worms?" it curiously grins.
"Just get them in style, with a splash and a cause!"
The owls roll their eyes, "Not the same old spins."

Fireflies twinkle, like stars in a chat,
"Did you hear the rumor about that old tree?"
Amidst the sweet scent, the breeze simply sat,
Chuckling softly at all of the glee.

So let's enjoy chats with a splash of delight,
As the moon keeps a secret known to the night.

Chants of the Changing Tides

As the sea calls out, splashing and singing,
Clams join the chorus, with notes full of glee.
Sand dollars bobble, their coins 'roundly swinging,
While the dolphins giggle, "Well, isn't this free?"

Crabs strut a dance, with their claws in the air,
"Who wore it better, the surf or the shell?"
The gulls laugh aloud, floating without a care,
"Please keep the jokes coming, we're under your spell!"

The tides have their tales, with each rise and fall,
Taking a dip in the heart of the show.
The seaweed's a jester, speaking to all,
With a hearty performance, there's much left to grow.

So let's join the wave, in this playful ballet,
'Cause the sea knows the magic of each sunny day.

The Dance of Fragrant Blooms

Flowers giggle softly, as breezes embrace,
Petals pirouette in a charming ballet.
Bees buzz a tune in this riotous space,
Sipping on nectar, in a whimsical way.

"Did you see that rose? Such charm and finesse!
But watch out for thorns that jest with the best!"
Lilies chime in, "We offer a mess,
With pollen confetti—come join the wild fest!"

The garden's a party, a fragrant affair,
Sunflowers tower, twirling high with delight.
With butterflies giggling, swirling up in the air,
They flutter and flip with a grand sense of height.

So let's dance with the blooms, under light's twinkling beams,
For the garden of laughter is truly our dreams.

Timeless Embrace of Ocean Spray

The ocean's kiss is cold and bright,
It splashes on my nose, what a sight!
I duck and dodge, like a clumsy clown,
With every wave, I tumble down.

Seagulls laugh, they mock my fall,
I wonder if they've seen it all.
With sandy toes and salty hair,
At least I'll leave without a care!

My drink is tipping, it's such a shame,
The jellyfish are part of the game.
They float on past, so carefree too,
While I just hope for less of their goo!

Oh, ocean breeze, you frolic and tease,
You're the jester dressed in seaweed leaves.
I'll chase the waves with a merry grin,
And dance around that barrel again!

Veils of Mist in Paradise

The fog rolls in, a sneak attack,
I lose my way, can't find the snack.
With every mist, I sense a cheer,
Is that a voice or random deer?

Palm trees swaying with comic style,
They wave and laugh, it's worth a while.
I trip on roots, oh what a mess,
I blame the breeze, I must confess!

Bananas giggle, coconuts chime,
At this rate, I'll lose track of time.
On this silly island, I'll take a break,
But not before a tropical shake!

A parrot squawks a funny tune,
He tells me jokes under the moon.
In misty veils, we twirl and sway,
Life's a party, let's laugh and play!

Tales from the Boughs of Life

A monkey swings, with joy and flair,
He steals my hat, and doesn't care!
I chase him up, but lose my grip,
Now I'm stuck on this wild trip!

The tree trunk hums a quirky song,
While squirrels giggle all day long.
What's in the shade, a coconut feast?
Or just a nutty, frolicking beast?

Clouds above are forming frowns,
Throwing down their rain-drop crowns.
With every splash, I cannot frown,
As laughter echoes all around.

Oh how the branches love to sway,
They cheer me on in this crazy play.
In tales of giggles and treehouse fun,
Our wild adventures have just begun!

The Quiet Lull of Water

In a pond so calm, I dip my toe,
The fish come up to say hello!
With a splash and wiggle, they tease my feet,
Who knew such fun was this simple treat?

The lily pads dance, so light and airy,
While frogs croak jokes, some quite scary!
They leap and bound with utmost grace,
But trip on reeds at a merry pace.

The gentle ripples tell tales so grand,
Of all the mischief that's simply planned.
Each bubble bursts with laughter near,
I can't help but chuckle, oh dear oh dear!

As the sun dips down, the moon takes flight,
In this watery world, everything feels right.
With giggles floating upon the pond,
I bid farewell to the night beyond!

Secrets on the Wind

The parrot squawks, a tale to share,
A lurking crab steals someone's chair.
Palm fronds nod with a giggle or two,
As the iguana plays peek-a-boo.

Coconuts drop with a plop and a thud,
A reminder to dodge, oh what a dud!
With sandy toes and giggles galore,
The heat brings laughter; who could ask for more?

The breeze carries secrets, cheeky and bright,
Every flip-flop squeaks, what a silly sight!
A thief in the night, a raccoon on the run,
In this tropical place, there's always some fun.

So roll in the waves, jump and dive,
Join in the party, feel so alive!
With every rustle and tickle of air,
Life's a comedy here, beyond compare.

Lullabies of the Palm Trees

The palm trees sway, a dance so absurd,
As squirrels debate who gets the last word.
A breeze tickles sandcastles, oh dear,
"Watch out!" cries a crab as he flies off in fear.

Lullabies sung by frogs on a log,
While a lizard sits, looking like a smug hog.
Starfish giggle in a tidal embrace,
As hula-hoop shells twirl in a wild race.

The sea whispers softly, a chuckle or two,
A dolphin leaps high, just to tease you.
With laughter and splashes, the day drifts away,
In this sunny kingdom, come out to play!

So close your eyes tight, let dreams take their flight,
Tomorrow brings more joy, from morning till night.
With giggles and wiggles, life's never a bore,
In the land of coconuts, we'll laugh evermore.

Murmurs Through the Mangroves

The mangroves murmur, "What's that sound?"
A fish jumps up, then flops right down.
Crabs in a conga line dance on the sand,
Their little claws waving, oh isn't life grand?

A frog croaks a joke, all ears perked high,
While fireflies flash, like twinkling stars in the sky.
With each gentle sway of the rhythmic tide,
Laughter erupts as friends collide.

The breeze carries tales of a crabby old snail,
Who dreamed he could dance, but just left a trail.
Coconut hats bob on heads oh so proud,
In this silly assembly, laughter's allowed!

So join in the fun as the sun starts to set,
With a jig and a wiggle, it's the best time yet.
In the heart of the mangroves, joy takes its stand,
With comedy blooming across this grand land.

Serenade of the Sea Salt

The sea salt sings to the surfers and fish,
With a symphony of giggles, oh what a dish!
Seagulls squawk, jesters in flight,
While turtles race slowly, what a comical sight!

Wave after wave brings on label mishaps,
A beach ball bounces, and a swimmer just flaps.
The tide draws back, revealing some loot,
A flip-flop and seashell caught in pursuit.

Giant umbrellas argue who gets the most sun,
While kids build castles and run just for fun.
With jellyfish wiggling, they giggle and sway,
In the melody of laughter, we'll play every day!

So gather around as the sun starts to dip,
Let's tell silly stories on this sandy trip.
With salty air tickling our cheeks, oh so bright,
This serenade of laughter lasts deep into night.

Dreams Carried by the Sea Breeze

A crab danced on the sandy floor,
With a top hat and a polished claw.
He promised me a feast of scallops bright,
But served me only seaweed in the light.

Seagulls cackled, wearing shades of blue,
Complaining 'bout the lack of a good view.
They played poker on a driftwood board,
Betting shells and dreaming of a shore ward.

The tide brought in some fish in a tie,
They looked so sharp, I'd swear they could fly.
I asked them where they were combing their scales,
They chuckled and whispered of 'oceanic tales.'

In the nightlife sun, the dolphins all pranced,
Claiming they'd win a swimming dance.
But tripped on a wave, they all took a dive,
And laughed as they splashed—what a way to thrive!

Whispered Hopes of the Lagoon

The flamingos lined up, all in pink,
Planning a party, ready to wink.
But slipped on mud, much to their dismay,
They flapped and screamed, 'What happened today?'

A turtle in shades lounged with a grin,
Counting his wrinkles, where to begin?
He said, 'Don't hurry, just take it slow!'
And then dozed off while the currents flow.

Dragonflies buzzed with tales of the breeze,
Spinning wild stories with effortless ease.
One claimed he met a mermaid named Sue,
But on closer look, it's the pond's water crew.

The lily pads hosted a dance on their leaves,
To tunes of croaking and soft, swaying sheaves.
Except for one frog who forgot his moves,
He leaped with a splash, wearing mismatched grooves!

Ocean's Tender Embrace

The whales hum songs that tickle the sea,
As fish swim by, laughing with glee.
With every splash, they giggle and play,
Mixing sea foam with the sun's bright ray.

A lobster in glasses debated his fate,
While a clam took selfies, thinking it great.
They plotted to start a marine fashion show,
But the fashion police were a fast-seeking flow!

Coral reefs hosted a tea party grand,
With starfish gossiping, hand in hand.
'The current said this; the tide just did that!'
And all the sea creatures wore a clever hat.

The barnacles gathered for some gossip and bread,
Spinning rumors they all claimed were well-bred.
And when asked to leave, they just wouldn't budge,
Saying, 'What's the rush? We are ocean's grudge!'

Aromas of Dusk in Paradise

At sunset, the coconuts started to sway,
With a mocktail party at the end of the day.
They served up jokes with every sweet sip,
And a punchline from a friendly banana ship.

The sun, in gold, made the palms clatter,
As monkeys swung by with a chatter-chatter.
They lost all their hats in a wind-blown burst,
And laughed so hard, quenching their thirst.

Tiki torches flickered, casting shadows galore,
While pineapples played limbo on the shore.
'The more we bend, the taller we stand!'
And they rolled in the sand, quite a sight so grand!

The evening breeze tossed confetti of leaves,
As the stars blinked down, like mischievous thieves.
But the island folks knew the night's true delight,
Was dancing and laughing under moon's silver light!

www.ingramcontent.com/pod-product-compliance
Lightning Source LLC
Chambersburg PA
CBHW052221090526
44585CB00015BA/1439